JUMP INTO SPORTS

Gymnastics

By Cynthia Amoroso

Gymnastics is a fun sport to watch. A gymnast must be strong and **flexible**.

Gymnasts use many skills when they compete.

Gymnasts practice in gyms with special equipment. Mats on the floor help protect gymnasts from getting hurt if they fall.

Being a gymnast takes a lot of practice.

Girls perform on the **uneven bars** and the **vault**. They also compete on the **balance beam** and the floor exercise.

The balance beam is very narrow. Gymnasts lose points if they fall off.

Boys perform on the vault and the floor exercise. They also use the **parallel bars**, the horizontal bar, the **pommel horse**, and the rings.

The rings are 9 feet (2.7 m) above the floor.

Gymnasts warm up before they begin. This helps to keep them from getting hurt.

Gymnasts put chalk on their hands to keep from getting hurt.

Gymnasts do different movements to show their balance. They learn **tumbling** skills.

Gymnasts practice flips and handstands.

Gymnasts also learn jumps and leaps. Some leap so well, it looks like they are flying!

It is important for gymnasts to point their toes.

Some gymnasts learn difficult skills. They can flip and twist. They practice spins and twirls.

Difficult tricks might get a gymnast more points.

Gymnasts show their strength and balance. At a **meet**, judges give them scores for each event.

Judges watch as a gymnast performs.

When the meet is over, the gymnasts with the best scores are the winners!

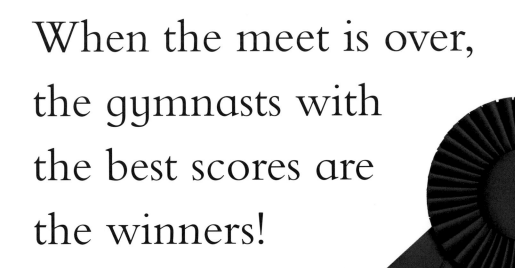

Gymnasts learn many poses and movements.

Glossary

balance beam (BAL-uhnss BEEM): A balance beam is a narrow rail that gymnasts perform a routine on. The gymnasts lose points for falling off the balance beam.

flexible (FLEK-suh-bull): To be flexible is to be able to bend. Gymnasts stretch their muscles to become more flexible.

meet (MEET): A meet is an event athletes attend to compete. At a gymnastics meet, there are many events.

parallel bars (PA-ruh-lel BARZ): The parallel bars are two horizontal bars that are the same height. Male gymnasts perform swings and release movements on the parallel bars.

pommel horse (PAH-mull HORSS): The pommel horse is a padded form with two handles on top. Male gymnasts perform balancing and strength moves on the pommel horse.

tumbling (TUM-bling): Tumbling is when a gymnast does handsprings or other flips. Tumbling is an important gymnastics skill.

uneven bars (uhn-EE-vuhn BARZ): The uneven bars are two horizontal bars that are different heights. Female gymnasts perform on the uneven bars.

vault (VAWLT): In the vault event, the gymnast runs down a runway and vaults off of a padded form to perform twists and flips. Men and women compete on the vault.

To Find Out More

Books

Bray-Moffatt, Naia, and Blanche Howard.
I Love Gymnastics. New York: DK Publishing, 2005.

Kalman, Bobbie. *Gymnastics in Action*. New York:
Crabtree Publishing, 2002.

Schlegel, Elfi, and Claire Rose Dunn. *The Gymnastics
Book: The Young Performer's Guide to Gymnastics*. Buffalo,
NY: Firefly, 2001.

Worsley, Arlene. *For the Love of Gymnastics*. New York:
Weigl Publishers, 2006.

Web Sites

Visit our Web site for links about gymnastics:
childsworld.com/links

Note to Parents, Teachers, and Librarians: We routinely
verify our Web links to make sure they are safe and active
sites. So encourage your readers to check them out!

Index

About the Author

Cynthia Amoroso has worked as a high school English teacher and an elementary school teacher. She is currently the curriculum director for a Minnesota school district. Writing children's books is another way for her to continue her passion for sharing the written word with children. Cynthia is a frequent visitor to the children's section of bookstores and enjoys spending time with her many friends, family, and two daughters.

On the cover: Gymnastics is a great way to stay flexible and get in shape.

Published by The Child's World®
1980 Lookout Drive • Mankato, MN 56003-1705
800-599-READ • www.childsworld.com

ACKNOWLEDGMENTS
The Child's World®: Mary Berendes, Publishing Director
The Design Lab: Design and production
Red Line Editorial: Editorial direction

PHOTO CREDITS: Vyacheslav Osokin/Shutterstock Images, cover;
Sergey Abalentsev/iStockphoto, cover; Gavin MacVicar/iStockphoto, 3;
Rich Legg/iStockphoto, 5, 11; Jing Dao Hua/Shutterstock Images, 7; Big
Stock Photo, 8, 13, 15; Galina Barskaya/Shutterstock Images, 9; Brian
McEntire/iStockphoto, 17; Trevor Nielson/iStockphoto, 19; PhotoDisc,
20; Galina Barskaya/iStockphoto, 21

Printed in the United States of America in Mankato, Minnesota.
November 2009
F11460

LIBRARY OF CONGRESS CATALOGING-IN-PUBLICATION DATA
Amoroso, Cynthia.
  Gymnastics / by Cynthia Amoroso.
     p. cm. — (Jump into sports)
  Includes bibliographical references and index.
  ISBN 978-1-60253-370-7 (library bound : alk. paper)
  1. Gymnastics—Juvenile literature. I. Title. II. Series.
  GV461.3.A66 2009
  796.44—dc22   2009030728

All sports carry a certain amount of risk. To reduce the risk of injury while doing gymnastics, play at your own level, wear all safety gear, and use care and common sense. The publisher and author take no responsibility or liability for injuries resulting from doing gymnastics.